INDIAN

JEOPARDY!

Answers and Questions About Our State

by
Carole Marsh

This activity book has material which correlates with Indiana's Academic Standards. At every opportunity, we have tried to relate information to the History and Social Science, English, Science, Math, Civics, Economics, and Computer Technology Academic Standards. For additional information, go to our websites: **www.indianaexperience.com** or **www.gallopade.com**.

Gallopade is proud to be a member of these educational organizations and associations:

The Indiana Experience Series

The Indiana Experience! Paperback Book

My First Pocket Guide to Indiana!

The Big Indiana Reproducible Activity Book

The Indiana Coloring Book!

My First Book About Indiana!

Indiana Jeopardy: Answers and Questions About Our State

Indiana Jography: A Fun Run Through Our State

The Indiana Experience! Sticker Pack

The Indiana Experience! Poster/Map

Discover Indiana CD-ROM

Indiana "GEO" Bingo Game

Indiana "HISTO" Bingo Game

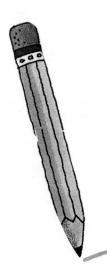

A Word... from the Author

The word is Jeopardy!

I'm sure you've all seen this popular game show. Actually, it's not much different from something kids seem to hate—the good, old-fashioned pop quiz! But how much more fun plain, boring questions and answers are when they're switcherooed into answers and questions!

I'm not trying to copy the actual Jeopardy game show format. I've just tried to use the reverse: "Here's the answer, now what's the question?" formula to make the facts about our state as interesting and intriguing as possible. Also, I think this format is a good double-check to see just how much all that history and geography is registering. Kids often know "facts" only in the memorized-order they learned them, which does not exactly = true knowledge, even if they do pass their tests.

The Answers and Questions on the next pages cover our state's history, geography, people, and much more. You can use the book in a variety of ways. If students want to read it on their own, they'll need to use a sheet of paper to cover the answers, oops!, I mean the questions. You could keep the book on the kitchen table and play Jeopardy while you eat breakfast. In the classroom, you could give the answers orally and let kids give the questions.

Whatever you do, keep score, have fun, let all ages participate, use wrong answers (I mean questions!) as the starting point for improved learning. Let kids have a chance to create their own Jeopardy answers and questions (It's much harder than it looks!). The only thing that should really be put in jeopardy are your frown muscles!

Carole Marsh

Indiana Trivia

Answer: The state capital of Indiana

QUESTION: What is Indianapolis?

Answer: Indiana's state motto

QUESTION: What is "The Crossroads of America"?

Answer: Indiana's nickname

QUESTION: What is the "Hoosier State"?

Answer: Indiana means this.

QUESTION: What is "land of the Indians"?

Answer: Indiana's state song

QUESTION: What is "On the Banks of the Wabash, Far Away"?

Indiana
All Around Our State

Answer: Fertile rolling plains located in Central Indiana

QUESTION: What is the Tipton Till?

Answer: State on Indiana's eastern border

QUESTION: What is Ohio?

Answer: The highest point in Indiana was named this by the General Assembly on July 1, 1993.

QUESTION: What is Hoosier High Point?

Answer: State on Indiana's northern border

QUESTION: What is Michigan?

Answer: Indiana's western border state

QUESTION: What is Illinois?

Hurry! I'm next.

This Land is Our Land

Answer: High ridges formed by melting glaciers

QUESTION: What are moraines?

Answer: Indiana's northwest border touches this Great Lake.

QUESTION: What is Lake Michigan?

Answer: One of the largest dunes on Lake Michigan's shore, it is called the "smoking dune" because the sand blowing off the top looks like wisps of smoke.

QUESTION: What is Mount Baldy?

Answer: River that forms Indiana's southern border

QUESTION: What is the Ohio River?

Answer: It is the largest natural lake in the state.

QUESTION: What is Lake Wawasee?

Indiana
Early Days

Answer: French explorer who was the first European to set foot in Indiana in 1679

QUESTION: Who was René-Robert Cavelier, Sieur de La Salle?

Answer: The first permanent settlement in Indiana, it was established by Jesuit missionaries around 1732.

QUESTION: What was Vincennes?

Answer: On July 13, 1787, Congress established this which included Indiana, Ohio, Michigan, Illinois, Wisconsin, and part of Minnesota.

QUESTION: What was the Northwest Territory?

Answer: British fort built in 1763 in Vincennes

QUESTION: What was Fort Sackville?

Answer: Territory established in 1800 which included Indiana, Illinois, Wisconsin, and parts of Minnesota and Michigan

QUESTION: What was the Indiana Territory?

Indiana
Patriotic People

Answer: First territorial governor of Indiana, ninth president of the U.S., and a hero of the Battle of Tippecanoe

QUESTION: Who was William Henry Harrison?

Answer: Army officer born in Liberty who commanded the Army of the Potomac during the Civil War

QUESTION: Who was Ambrose Burnside?

Answer: He planted apple seeds as he walked through Ohio, Indiana, and Illinois territories.

QUESTION: Who was John Chapman (Johnny Appleseed)?

Answer: Astronaut who commanded the first spaceflight to orbit the moon

QUESTION: Who is Frank Borman?

Answer: Governor and U.S. senator who raised money to support Indiana troops

QUESTION: Who was Oliver Hazard Perry Throck Morton?

Indiana
Conflicts and Hostilities

Answer: A war, which started in 1754, that was really between England and France, but Indians were involved on both sides

QUESTION: What was the French and Indian War?

Answer: He led the American soldiers who defeated the English and captured Fort Sackville during the Revolutionary War.

QUESTION: Who was George Rogers Clark?

Answer: General "Mad Anthony" Wayne led the soldiers who defeated the Miami Indians at this battle in 1794.

QUESTION: What was the Battle of Fallen Timbers?

Answer: After losing this 1811 battle, the Indians of the Great Lakes were no longer united in their efforts to stop settlers.

QUESTION: What was the Battle of Tippecanoe?

Answer: More than 10,000 Hoosiers died during this war in the 1940s.

QUESTION: What was World War II?

Indiana
Real Estate

Answer: City that is home to the University of Notre Dame

QUESTION: What is South Bend?

Answer: City that is home to the world's largest high school fieldhouse and to the Indiana Basketball Hall of Fame Museum

QUESTION: What is New Castle?

Answer: Fossil beds lie in plain site in this state park near Madison.

QUESTION: What is Falls of the Ohio State Park?

Answer: A cave near Leavenworth is home to the largest underground limestone "mountain."

QUESTION: What is Wyandotte Cave?

Answer: This central Indiana county has 32 19th-century covered bridges, more than any other county in the nation.

QUESTION: What is Parke County?

Indiana
A Date To Remember

Monday Tuesday Wednesday Thursday Friday Saturday Sunday

		1	2	3	4	5

Answer: The date on which Indiana became the 19th state

QUESTION: What is December 11, 1816?

Answer: In 1825, it became the state capital.

QUESTION: What is Indianapolis?

Answer: U.S. Steel planned this city in 1906 to serve its steel-making plants which started production in 1909.

QUESTION: What is Gary?

Answer: In 1894, a Kokomo resident test drove the first gasoline-powered, clutch-driven automobile with an electric ignition.

QUESTION: Who was Elwood Haynes?

Answer: The road that opened in 1956 and joined the western and eastern borders of the state

QUESTION: What is the Indiana Toll Road?

Indiana
Scholarly Smarts

Answer: In 1816, this state document was the first in the nation to provide for free public schools for students from elementary school to college.

QUESTION: What is the constitution?

Answer: The social reformer and his community who introduced educational experiments such as nursery schools, trade schools, and boys and girls in classes together

QUESTION: Who was Robert Owen and the New Harmony community?

Answer: Children between the ages of seven and this age are required to attend school by Indiana law.

QUESTION: What is 18?

Answer: Founded near South Bend in 1842, it is one of the top Catholic universities in the world.

QUESTION: What is the University of Notre Dame?

Answer: Originally known as the Terre Haute School of Industrial Science, it was established on September 10, 1874.

QUESTION: What is the Rose-Hulman Institute of Technology?

Answer: The first long-distance auto race was held here on May 30, 1911.

QUESTION: What is the Indianapolis Motor Speedway?

Answer: Indiana University swimmer who won seven gold medals in the 1972 Olympics

QUESTION: Who is Mark Spitz?

Answer: She started selling her cosmetics door-to-door in 1905 and became one of the nation's first women millionaires.

QUESTION: Who was Madame C.J. Walker (Sarah Walker)?

Answer: Indiana's first newspaper was published in 1804 at Vincennes.

QUESTION: What was the *Indiana Gazette*?

Answer: Berne is home to one of the largest congregations of this religious group in the nation.

QUESTION: What are Mennonites?

We're number one!

Grown and Made in Indiana

Answer: Indiana's leading crop

QUESTION: What is corn?

Answer: Herbs used in chewing gum, they grow in the marshy soil of the northeastern lake country.

QUESTION: What are peppermint and spearmint?

Answer: Indianapolis grocer who opened a canning company after he found customers liked his old family recipe for pork and beans.

QUESTION: Who is Gilbert Van Camp?

Answer: Indiana is the nation's number one producer of this domesticated fowl.

QUESTION: What are ducks?

Answer: Indiana's most valuable livestock product

QUESTION: What are hogs?

What are you bringing to the picnic?

Pork 'n' beans!

Indiana
Music and Film

Answer: He published his first song at the age of 11 and is known for his many musicals and hits, including "I've Got You under My Skin" and "My Heart Belongs to Daddy."

QUESTION: Who was Cole Porter?

Answer: Seymour singer and songwriter whose hits have included "Jack and Diane" and "Authority Song"

QUESTION: Who is John Mellencamp?

Answer: Indianapolis television news anchor who is host of *Dateline NBC*

QUESTION: Who is Jane Pauley?

Answer: The late-night television talk show host who is from Indianapolis

QUESTION: Who is David Letterman?

Answer: This 1950s movie star from Marion starred in *East of Eden* and *Rebel Without a Cause*, and was killed in a car accident at the age of 24.

QUESTION: Who was James Dean?

Ready for your 15 minutes?

Yeah!

Indiana
Laudable Landmarks

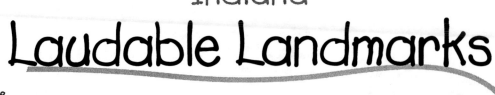

Answer: Indiana city once known as the "Circus Capital of the World" that is home to the Circus City Museum

QUESTION: What is Peru?

Answer: Fountain City house that was once an important stop on the Underground Railroad

QUESTION: What is the Levi Coffin House?

Answer: Noblesville attraction that is a 30-building living history museum which takes people back to the early 1800s

QUESTION: What is Conner Prairie Pioneer Settlement?

Answer: Famous buildings in this Ohio River city include the Shrewsbury House, the J.F.D. Lanier Mansion, and the Sullivan House.

QUESTION: What is Madison?

Answer: Stadium in West Lafayette that is home to Purdue University's football team

QUESTION: What is the Ross Ade Stadium?

Indiana
Weather or Not

Answer: These funnel-shaped columns of air that swirl very fast and destroy everything in their path hit Indiana in the spring.

QUESTION: What are tornadoes?

Answer: The average amount of this form of precipitation is 20 inches (51 centimeters), but can be as much as 100 inches (254 centimeters) in northern Indiana.

QUESTION: What is snow?

Answer: The average temperature for this season ranges from 35°F (2°C) in south Indiana to 25°F (-4°) in northern Indiana.

QUESTION: What is winter?

Answer: The season when the average temperature is 73°F (23°C) in the north to 78°F (26°C) in the south

QUESTION: What is summer?

Answer: The river that flooded in 1937 killing dozens of people and destroying towns

QUESTION: What is the Ohio River?

Indiana
Scavenger Hunt

Answer: The family of this U.S. president moved from Kentucky and settled in Spencer County in 1816.

QUESTION: Who was Abraham Lincoln?

Answer: The Indiana region that is home to the cities of Hammond, Whiting, East Chicago, and Gary

QUESTION: What is the Calumet region?

Answer: The Root Glass Company in Terre Haute designed the unique glass bottle used by this soft drink company

QUESTION: What is Coca-Cola?

Answer: The monument in the center of Indianapolis that is a shrine to those who died defending the United States

QUESTION: What is the Soldiers and Sailors Monument?

Answer: The national forest in south-central Indiana where Patoka Lake is located

QUESTION: What is the Hoosier National Forest?

Answer: The state bird

QUESTION: What is the Cardinal?

Answer: The state tree is also known as the yellow poplar.

QUESTION: What is the Tulip Tree?

Answer: This large flower that comes in shades of red, pink, or white is the state flower.

QUESTION: What is a Peony?

Answer: The Empire State Building in New York City and the Washington National Cathedral in Washington, D.C. are made from Indiana's state rock.

QUESTION: What is Limestone?

Answer: The state river's name comes from the Indian word for limestone.

QUESTION: What is the Wabash River?

Indiana Counties

Answer: The number of counties in Indiana

QUESTION: What is 92?

Answer: The Indianapolis 500 is held in this county.

QUESTION: What is Marion County?

Answer: The county where the University of Notre Dame in South Bend is located

QUESTION: What is St. Joseph County?

Answer: In this county, the Tippecanoe Battlefield State Memorial is located near the town of Battle Ground.

QUESTION: What is Tippecanoe County?

Answer: Angel Mounds, an important historic site, is located just outside of Evansville in this county and has 11 earthen platform mounds built by the Moundbuilders.

QUESTION: What is Vanderburgh County?

Answer: Wildlife experts are teaching these waterfowl to migrate by having them follow an airplane from Ontario, Canada to southern Indiana.

QUESTION: What are trumpeter swans?

Answer: Every Fourth of July, a small town in southwest Indiana sponsors a race for cockroaches.

QUESTION: What is Roachdale?

Answer: A mammal that is an excellent swimmer and has a fun-loving reputation

QUESTION: What is the otter?

Answer: Endangered in Indiana, this bird has a yellow head and neck and a black body with white markings on the wings.

QUESTION: What is the yellow-headed blackbird?

Answer: The largest animal left in Indiana's forests, they are one of the best-known and most admired animals.

QUESTION: What is the deer?

Indiana
Indian Powwow

Answer: Chief of the Miami tribe who was defeated at the Battle of Fallen Timbers

QUESTION: Who was Chief Little Turtle?

Answer: Shawnee chief who tried to organize the Indian resistance against settlers

QUESTION: Who was Tecumseh?

Answer: Name given to Tecumseh's brother, Tenskwatawa, who was defeated at the Battle of Tippecanoe

QUESTION: Who was the Shawnee Prophet?

Answer: Early Indian people who built the Angel Mounds near Evansville

QUESTION: Who were the Mississipians?

Answer: The Eiteljorg Museum of American Indians and Western Art in this city gives a glimpse of Native American culture in Indiana.

QUESTION: What is Indianapolis?

Indiana
Prestigious Politics

☆ ☆ ☆ ☆ ☆ ☆ ☆ ☆ ☆ ☆ ☆ ☆ ☆ ☆ ☆

Answer: Indiana has only had two of these—the first was adopted in 1816 and the second was approved by voters in 1851.

QUESTION: What is a state constitution?

Answer: The age Indiana residents must reach before they can register to vote.

QUESTION: What is 18?

Answer: Indiana's top elected official can only serve two consecutive terms in office.

QUESTION: Who is the governor?

Answer: Name given to the state's senate and house of representatives

QUESTION: What is the General Assembly?

Answer: The state spends most of its money on this.

QUESTION: What is education?

Indiana
Lofty Leaders

Answer: He served as vice-president with President George Bush from 1989 to 1993.

QUESTION: Who is Dan Quayle?

Answer: He served as the 23rd president of the U.S. from 1889 to 1893.

QUESTION: Who was Benjamin Harrison?

Answer: He served as a representative to the U.S. Congress and later as vice-president of the U.S. from 1869-1873

QUESTION: Who is Schuyler Colfax?

Answer: Indiana Republican who ran for president against Franklin D. Roosevelt in 1940 and lost.

QUESTION: Who was Wendell Willkie?

Answer: He served as mayor of Gary from 1967 to 1987 and was one of the first African-American mayors of a big city.

QUESTION: Who is Richard Hatcher?

Indiana
Statehood

Answer: The U.S. president who signed Congress' resolution for Indiana statehood in 1816

QUESTION: Who was James Madison?

Answer: City declared the state capital when Indiana became a state.

QUESTION: What was Corydon?

Answer: Before Indiana joined the Union, there were this many states.

QUESTION: What is 18 (Indiana's order of admission was 19th)?

Answer: First governor of the state of Indiana

QUESTION: Who was Jonathan Jennings?

Answer: When Indianapolis became the state capital in 1825, the government set up its offices in this building until the state capitol building was built.

QUESTION: What is the Marion County Courthouse?

Indiana
The Hoosier State

Answer: A museum in Indianapolis that is the world's largest museum devoted to kids

QUESTION: What is the Children's Museum of Indianapolis?

Answer: He won a Pulitzer Prize in 1944 for his news reports from the field during World War II and was killed during the Okinawa campaign.

QUESTION: Who was Ernie Pyle?

Answer: Controversial Indiana University basketball coach known for his teams' success on the court and in the classroom.

QUESTION: Who is Bob Knight?

Answer: Head football coach at Notre Dame who posted a record of 105 wins, 12 losses, and 5 ties from 1918 to 1930

QUESTION: Who was Knute Rockne?

Answer: An All-American guard at Purdue, he is one of the most successful coaches in basketball history and led UCLA to 10 national championships in the 1960s and 1970s.

QUESTION: Who was John Wooden?

Indiana
Flag Facts

Answer: They adopted the state flag in 1917.

QUESTION: What is the General Assembly?

Answer: The flag features this symbol and golden stars on a blue background.

QUESTION: What is a flaming golden torch?

Answer: The outer circle of 13 stars stand for these.

QUESTION: What are the original 13 states?

Answer: The star directly above the flame of the torch represents this.

QUESTION: What is Indiana?

Answer: This symbol represents liberty and enlightenment.

QUESTION: What is the torch?

I pledge allegiance...

...to the flag...

Indiana
Arts & Artists

Answer: Dancer and choreographer who blends classical ballet, tap dance, and popular social dances

QUESTION: Who is Twyla Tharp?

Answer: The Indianapolis Symphony Orchestra performs in this restored theater.

QUESTION: What is the Hilbert Circle Theatre?

Answer: Sculptor Robert Clark changed his name to this in order to show his Hoosier pride.

QUESTION: Who is Robert Indiana?

Answer: Most famous of the Brown County artists who painted nature scenes inspired by the hills of southern Indiana

QUESTION: Who was Theodore C. (T.C.) Steele?

Answer: William Forsyth, Otto Stark, and John Bundy were artists known for celebrating nature in romantic landscapes.

QUESTION: Who were the Hoosier Group?

Answer: A standout at Springs Valley High School and Indiana State University, he went on to a successful professional basketball career with the Boston Celtics.

QUESTION: Who is Larry Bird?

Answer: Thirteen of these cross Indiana, more than any other state.

QUESTION: What are interstate highways?

Answer: This religious group arrived in Indiana around 1807 and established the town of Richmond and opened Earlham College.

QUESTION: What is the Society of Friends (Quakers)?

Answer: More people of this profession graduate from Indiana University than any other school in the country.

QUESTION: What are medical doctors?

Answer: The Crystal Palace, an underground room, is located in this cave.

QUESTION: What is Marengo Cave?

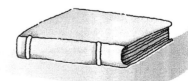

Indiana
Literary Laureates

Answer: He was known as the Hoosier Poet.

QUESTION: Who was James Whitcomb Riley?

Answer: A major general during the Civil War, he wrote *Ben-Hur*.

QUESTION: Who was Lew Wallace?

Answer: Her novel, *Friendly Persuasion*, tells about the struggles of an Indiana Quaker family during the Civil War.

QUESTION; Who was Jessamyn West?

Answer: He won the Pulitzer Prize for fiction for these novels—*The Magnificent Ambersons* and *Alice Adams*.

QUESTION: Who was Booth Tarkington?

Answer: Writer best known for the sentimental novels *Freckles* and *The Girl of the Limberlost*

QUESTION: Who was Gene Stratton-Porter?

Naturally Indiana

Answer: The mineral that comes from strip mines in southwestern Indiana

QUESTION: What is coal?

Answer: Quarries in south-central Indiana supply huge chunks of this stone for buildings.

QUESTION: What is limestone?

Answer: These can be found in French Lick, West Baden, and Martinsville.

QUESTION: What are mineral springs?

Answer: The trees that provide the Amish with the sap used to make maple syrup

QUESTION: What are maple trees?

Answer: The winds blowing off of Lake Michigan formed this protected area.

QUESTION: What is the Indiana Dunes National Lakeshore?

Hello up there!

Answer: Cartoonist who created the "Garfield" comic strip

QUESTION: Who is Jim Davis?

Answer: Cave near Bedford that is one of the 10 largest caves in the world

QUESTION: What is Bluespring Cavern?

Answer: Day celebrated across the state on December 11, the anniversary of statehood

QUESTION: What is Indiana Day?

Answer: The Popcorn Festival, held the Saturday after Labor Day, celebrates the treat grown on 17,000 acres (6,879.9 hectares) around this town.

QUESTION: What is Valparaiso?

Answer: Nature preserve near Bainbridge that is home to a blue heron rookery and what is believed to be the largest sugar maple tree in the world

QUESTION: What is the Big Walnut State Nature Preserve?

Well— here we are.

Yeah!